Denise—

Continue

that so many are searching

for. I'm so thankful you found

your voice in the midst of the

storm.

Lisa Hall*

Nov. 14, 2016

The Cuts Don't Hurt Anymore: From Abuse to Abundance

©2016 Lisa Halls

Email To:

Lisa Halls

Myvoiceisreal@gmail.com

Social Media: @Lisa_Halls

ISBN-13: 978-1537327235

ISBN-10: 1537327232

Published in The United States of America

The Cuts Don't Hurt Anymore

From Abuse to Abundance!

-Lisa Halls-

This book is dedicated to my amazing children, continue to follow your dreams, as nothing is impossible.

This book is also dedicated to my dear friend Tommy Roberts, thank you for believing in me and encouraging me to write and share my story.

Table of Contents

Foreward
John McClung, Jr. 9

Chapter One
Adapting to Abuse...11

Chapter Two
The Breakdown from Abuse...17

Chapter Three
Understanding The Abuse..31

Chapter Four
Surviving The Abuse..37

Chapter Five
Excelling, The Final Cut...65

About The Author
Lisa Halls...71

Foreward

Author John McClung Jr.

Over the years, I have been fortunate to share and read stories of many people who have crossed my path. I am a businessman, entrepreneur, Best Selling Author and writing has been a passion for me. As I read through the pages of this wonderful book, I realized the voice that was sharing the heartfelt stories had been silent for many years. The Cuts Don't Hurt No More is a book that speaks volumes to the emotional, personal and physical life of many people who have been dealing with the scars in their life they don't want anyone to know about. Ms. Lisa Halls has opened up her heart and soul for the world to not only see, but also for them to recognize there is a part of us that can identify with the pain, the hurts, the challenges and eventually the triumphs that can bring us from whatever abuse we go through to abundance. I know that she has been truly given a purpose designed by God to share her personal struggles that hindered her from being the person she was called to be and in this book she expresses her journey in ways that grab, holds and captivates you as you find yourself hanging on every word. This book will change, impact and add value to many lives that have the opportunity to read it. As I shared with Lisa, "What you say and write may not be for everybody, but it is for somebody and when that somebody reads it, everybody will know it." Be that somebody! Your life will never be the same. I can't be more proud of the work she has consistently dedicated herself to in creating this wonderfully well put together book. I am honored to have been chosen to pen this foreword and I pray that all who share in this wonderful chapter in her life understand "THE CUTS DON'T HURT NO MORE" and she has risen from the 'ABUSE TO ABUNDANCE'

Congratulations Lisa Halls!

John McClung Jr

CEO/Founder of I AM A TESTIMONY CLOTHING

Amazon Best Selling Author

Life Messenger/Trainer/Coach

Adapting to Abuse

CHAPTER ONE

Never forget that walking away from something unhealthy is brave, even if you stumble a little on your way out the door. It was a Saturday evening around 8 o'clock in the summertime. I remember when I was ten years old, my brother, sister and I were sitting in the living room watching a movie together. My father came home after a long day, walked in the door and my mom said, "Hey Honey, how was your day?" My father upset from his long day walked in the door and started yelling at my mom. My mom sent my siblings and I to our room to play, so we didn't have to see the fighting. Being the oldest, I did everything I could to keep my brother and sister occupied and somewhat quiet. They were so little at this time. It was close to our bedtime. My mom came in and got us ready for bed, tucked us in bed, kissed, and told us she loved us and shut the lights off. Have you ever been so scared that your heart beats fast, and tears start flowing because you don't have any control over the situation? I remember laying in my bed, with my legs curled up to my chest, tears streaming down my face wishing the fighting would stop. I could hear my mom crying and a couple of times saying to my dad "DON'T HIT ME AGAIN!" Would you have gotten out of bed? I wanted too, I wanted to defend my mom, but didn't in fear. I just stayed in bed praying to God that the fighting would stop, that my dad would go for a drive until he was cooled off, and then come back home and everything would be content for the night. I remember lying in bed, making sure I stayed awake, to make sure my mom was alright before I went to sleep. This happened many nights, unfortunately. My family lived a couple streets down from my grandma at the time. I can remember many nights, my mom would pack us kids up in the car and drive over to her home for the night, to get away from the fighting, and have a peaceful night's sleep. My parents were married for twelve years, and I know they both thought things would get better, and easier.

We had some good times that I remember as a child, but a lot of it is remembered with the fighting and contention. I know my parents didn't want a broken family and they stayed together and tried to make it work for so long. This was a normal routine in my family.

Just as despair can come to one, only from other human beings, hope, too, can be given to one only by other human beings. At the young age of twelve, my parents divorced. I remember having so many mixed emotions going on at that time. I was sad my dad wouldn't be in our home anymore, but I was relieved I wouldn't have to hear my mom cry anymore, or hear the fighting. I know that being a single mom was extremely difficult for my mom. As it is for all single parents. My mom had a lot of support from family to help with my siblings and I. We were able to see my dad every other weekend. That was challenging to adapt to since we saw him every day after school and work. When my parents separated and divorced, I looked after my siblings often. Have you ever or anyone you know, felt like you were a single mom at the age of ten? How did you feel? Looking after my younger siblings, making sure they were fed, cleaned up after them and took care of them, was challenging at times. I felt a lot of responsibility was placed on me at a young age, but I also knew the help my mom was in need of. Knowing we were safe, and she could go to work and come home and things would be taken care of. The transition was difficult for all of us. I missed my dad a lot. At this time, I didn't know how it would affect me in the future. I still love my dad a lot, my dad

13

and I have a great relationship now. I was inspired by a friend to write my story.

As we were talking on the phone, he asked what has been going on in my life since we last spoke many, many years ago. When I summarized what I've been through, he encouraged me to write. I so wanted to help someone. I wanted people to know what it's like to be transparent. As my children wanted to be transparent as well. I learned to adapt to the "norm" at a young age. We all had to learn to adapt. At least at that time in my life, I thought that was the way to live. I'm sure some have you had to adapt to a lifestyle of what you thought the norm was. Life has always had its ups and downs. You can either choose to accept what happens, move on and grow from your experiences, or you can allow it to take over your life blaming others for why your life has turned out the way you never imagined.

Reader Notes:

What ways were you able to adapt to a situation in your life, and triumph from it?

_____

_____

_____

_____

_____

_____

_____

_____

_____

_____

_____

_____

_____

_____

_____

_____

_____

_____

Breakdown to Abuse
CHAPTER TWO

He stripped away my self- worth, layer by layer until there was nothing left of my personality. Yet I never forgot about the girl who I used to be. She lived inside, my caged soul, waiting for the day I would set her free. Casting her light into my dark mind, hoping that I would see, flashes of a better life, glimpse of possibility. I was never alone because she believed in me. I quickly fell in what I thought was love, at an early age. I was Eighteen at this time. Shortly into the relationship I got pregnant, it was soon after high school. I wasn't prepared for the challenges of raising children; I just knew I wanted a baby. I remember the excitement I felt when I found out I was pregnant. Being married at that time wasn't important, I was going through challenges with my boyfriend at that time, and thought that of having a baby would bring us closer together. At an early age of nineteen, I was having my baby boy out of wedlock. The struggles and the stress only became stronger, because now I was bringing a baby into a relationship and this world. The pregnancy was hard, and I was sick most of it. But when my baby boy was born I was overjoyed, and my heart was full of unconditional love I had for him. As any new mother, I embraced every moment with my little one. Six weeks later I became pregnant again, this time with a baby girl. I remember feeling scared at this time. How was I going to raise two babies so close together? These thoughts raced through my head. The pregnancy with my little girl was much easier than my first pregnancy. I remember the joy I felt when the nurse placed her in my arms. Having two babies was quite challenging. My son started walking shortly after I was home from delivering my daughter. It felt like twins raising the two of them. Twenty months later I was delivering my third son.

Two babies were challenging but having three in diapers, life was crazy, wonderful, challenging, and sometimes stressful. I remember being home and feeling overwhelmed. My little ones were having a rough day, at that time like most women, I suffered from postpartum depression. I felt like my job as a mom, was being fulfilled completely. I couldn't stop crying. I received a phone call from a dear friend of mine and the words she said to me brought so much comfort. She said "You are important, and you matter. Your feelings matter, your voice matters. As she continued on, she said your life matters, your story matters. It will impact so many people one day. Then she said to me YOU MATTER!" So much comfort was brought to my heart and I felt a sense of calmness over me. I was with my kid's father for seven years married for four months. It was a sunny afternoon on Sunday, my kid's father said he was going to a friend's house. He didn't come home that evening or the next day. It was a couple of days later that I learned he wasn't coming back ever again. He had cheated on me and had secretly moved on with his life. I didn't learn until after he left that drugs had taken over his life.

The new life he was living, with his girlfriend and drugs, was not something I wanted my kids to be around. He chose to completely walk away from his family, and not be involved even from a distance with his children. He moved on with his life, having several more children. It was really hard for my children, having their dad leave their life. My children were really young at this time. I went from being a stay at home mom, to working full time. The transition was extremely difficult, as I really enjoyed staying home with my children.

Soon after my kid's father left us, I moved back home with my parents for a short time. It was temporary while getting back on my feet. I was grateful they opened their doors for my kids and myself to stay, while getting everything situated. During that time my car was stolen, public transportation was my only option. I remember having to wake up early every morning, to get my kids ready for daycare and myself ready for work. It was so cold outside.

I bundled my babies up and each morning we would set out on our journey, just in time to catch the bus on time to reach our destination. With three babies it was quite challenging but we did it. I was eventually able to get back on my feet and move into a small two-bedroom apartment. It was tight, but it was enough room for my kids and myself.

Fast forward two years later. On a cloudy day, I had taken my oldest son to the dentist office, and while sitting in the waiting area, I sparked conversation with a man waiting for his son as well. Through exchanging some information, we realized that our children were close to the same age. We had a lot in common, or so it seemed at the time. He asked me and my son to lunch that day, then we helped him move to a different house.

We soon started dating. Again fell in love quickly for many of the wrong reasons. Shortly into the relationship I became pregnant with my fourth child. I thought this was the relationship I've been waiting for. Things were really good for a while. I never imagined things would take a turn for the worst. I had no idea of the domestic abuse I would be experiencing, and the abuse my kids would go through.

It started with verbal abuse. He would constantly put me down in front of the children. Call me names, and threaten to kick me out of the house many times. I remember crying myself to sleep many nights. I was brainwashed for so many years with things being said like "no one will ever want you with four children. You know you can't make it without me." I allowed those thoughts to stay in my head for years. These thoughts created fear and loss of self-esteem. How was I going to raise four children on my own? Through the abuse my children and I experienced, I felt trapped and felt there was no way out. I was living in darkness and despair and I became really good at masking my pain in front of others. It was much easier for me to put a smile on my face and be happy in public, and cry behind closed doors. I learned at an early time in my relationship, I wasn't able to speak my mind. No matter what I said, I was never right. My opinion didn't matter. I learned to be silent, as it would start a fight if I offered my opinion at a time, so the best thing to do was to agree that my husband was always right. I often spoke for my children, so their answer and responses to my husband didn't set off a trigger. I WAS THE VOICE for my children. I would cry for my children for the pain I was causing them because at that time I thought I wasn't strong enough to walk away.

The behavior in my children shifted. They were angry. They fought and argued much more than normal. Slamming doors, yelling at each other. They shut down their communication a lot with me. I noticed behaviors of my children being more silent. Afraid to talk, or speak their mind. I noticed behaviors of my children being more silent. Afraid to talk, or speak their mind. As much as I tried getting through to them, I felt I kept hitting a wall. I couldn't figure out a way to reach them. I thought it was because of the abuse we were going through. Until I later learned that three out of four of my children were sexually abused by my stepson. They were raped and molested over and over again. I couldn't believe it. It was then that it all started coming together. Why they were so closed up and reserved. My husband and I work nights, so I wasn't aware that this was happening while we were away. My husband and I were either at work or asleep when he chose to attack my children. He also did it in the middle of the night when I was sleeping. He would sneak into my daughter's bedroom, while she was sleeping, and go under her sheets and touch her. He would put her up in a corner and he would rape her.

I can't imagine the pain that my children went through every single day, because of what they were experiencing, and not being able to tell anybody in fear of getting hurt more. I remember being asleep one night, and my daughter yelling at my step son, "GET OUT OF MY ROOM!" I jumped out of bed and ran into her room, to see what was going on. It was then that I found out what was happening. I was so sick to my stomach. I couldn't believe it. I yelled and screamed at him. How could he do this do my daughter! What the hell was going through his mind, and how did he think this was ok? I later learned that my boys were also victims, he would make threats to my children that if they spoke out and told anybody he would hurt them more. When I learned about this, I reported it to the Law Enforcement and later my stepson was removed out of my home. That night I told my oldest to pack some things as we were leaving in the morning, while my husband was sleeping. I scooped up my kids and we left on our journey.

I told my youngest child that we were going to the park for the day, knowing in my mind we would never return. This was the seventh time of me leaving. The first time I left, my husband I got into a fight, and like any other fight, he would tell me to leave. Not knowing this was how he dealt with his emotions when things got rough, it was easier to kick my kids and I out than to try to work through our problems. So we left. I went and stayed with a friend for a couple of days. He called and apologized, told me how sorry he was and wanted to make it work between us. I have never been one to give up, and watching my mom endure what she went through, I wasn't giving up. I was giving my all. My kids and I went back to him. Life would go well for a little while. Of course, they did! I gave in and went back to make it work. We had arguments every now and then, as all couples do. Blending families are at times quite challenging.

As time passed on, we got into another argument. It wasn't just a simple argument. It was a lot of him yelling and screaming at me. Usually consisted of him cursing me out. I wasn't allowed to voice what was on my mind. If I did, it would increase the tension, and add to the fight or cause another one after that initial one was done. Again he told us to leave. Each time I left, the fights got worse. What I was allowed to leave with lessoned. I left again. I didn't want any of the kids to continue hearing or witness the fighting. My heart hurt, as I thought this was the man I was spending the rest of my life with. Why did he keep giving up each time things got difficult? This time, I went and stayed with a cousin. Everyone told me often, I should leave, to walk away for good. I would be so much better off, but I didn't want to believe it. Even though times were challenging, I kept reminding myself.... This IS the man I'm spending my life with. After I left, the next couple of days he would call me. Crying and telling me again how sorry he was. He wanted to make it work. He would leave messages when I didn't answer, begging me to come back to him. Have you ever left a situation, thinking it was going to be the last time you be there, only to find yourself back in it again? I went back to him again. My kids were little during this time. I knew they understood what was going on. I drove back to his house, to attempt to make things work a third time. I was afraid of being alone. Afraid of raising four children on my own, and I really wanted this to work between us. I was able to be a stay at home mom, and the thought of having to go to work and leave my children at that time was something I couldn't imagine doing. I knew other families who took their kids to daycare, but if I could stay and do all I could to make it work, I was going to do it. Life was steady again for a while, until one day he came home from work. I had a long day with the kids, the house wasn't picked up to his approval and dinner wasn't done yet. Another argument started, and again after screaming and yelling, told me to leave. This time, I wasn't leaving with anything but my kids. He took the keys from me and told me to have a friend pick us up. I wasn't allowed to have a car. I didn't care at the time. I was so tired from all the fighting, I called a friend and she came and picked my kids and I up.

Again, the text messages starting coming. My phone rang constantly. There were many times, I would have to turn my phone off, just to have some peace, quiet and sanity. I was promised counseling and those things were going to get better. I was promised so many things, only to come back to broken promises. We never got counseling. The fighting continued. But

I was determined. I wasn't giving up. What could someone tell you or someone you know, that was in this situation? So many times I was told to leave. No one really understood what I was going through behind closed doors. If I could give you any advice, it would be to just listen. You can't offer any advice to leave. Just listen. Listen to what they are going through. That's truly what that person wants. Offer advice when they ask for it.

Reader Notes:

Think of a past situation that you held onto, why couldn't you let go?

_____

_____

_____

_____

_____

_____

_____

_____

_____

_____

_____

_____

_____

_____

_____

_____

_____

Understanding The Abuse
CHAPTER THREE

So many times I would leave and come back, with empty promises of we will get counseling, my stepson would be removed out of our home and things will get better, but things only got worse. He yelled at me, called me names and would tell me how worthless I was. He would say you're crazy, that never happened. You're so dramatic and sensitive. You must be confused again. Just calm down! Stop overreacting! He lived in denial often that he was never wrong. No matter the situation, he was always right according to him. It was a very dark world that I lived in for eight years. I would leave with my children and I would come back. Each time that I attempted to leave, he would take the keys to the car he would scream at me, and at times hold me against the wall telling me I wasn't leaving. There would be times, where he would hit me, other times he would hold his fist in the air towards my face and yell "Oh I could just hit you right now!" There were times I wish he would have, and many other times he did. With my kids behind him, my back against the wall, I knew this is not the life that I wanted to continue to live. I remember a couple of times my husband and I were in the room together, he threw me on the bed and raped me. Saying to me, "Is this how you like it?" With tears streaming down my face, crying and trying to fight him off of me, I prayed it would end soon. Once he would leave the house for a little while, I would get in the shower, let the water pour over me as I stood there and cried. What did I do to deserve this?

I didn't realize that I was causing so much heartache, and turmoil to my children staying in that relationship until after I left. The pain is so personal. No matter how many times my children told me to leave, I didn't. At the time, I didn't want to have another broken family. So I stayed and hoped that things would continue to get better, as they only got worse as time went on.

I did this back and forth, for six times before I finally said enough is enough, and I walked away the seventh time for good. I couldn't take the abuse any longer. I came to the realization that Enough Is Enough. I couldn't take what I was dealing with for so many years. I was tired of the yelling, the screaming, the fighting, and the abuse. I was exhausted. I couldn't keep my kids in this situation anymore. It was up to me to make sure they found their happiness again. My kids were scared to come home at times and later learned that even going to sleep at night was fearful for them. I couldn't allow my kids to live in fear. I was tired of crying myself to sleep at night. I was TIRED! I wanted my children to see that over time, I gave it my everything! I stuck it out, no matter how hard it was, and how painful the situation, I NEVER gave up. But when I learned of the abuse my children had faced, I had to leave. It was up to me to protect them from their predator.

I know there are many of you that have been in very challenging and hard situations, where you have told yourself, I've had enough. You did whatever you had to do to leave, and even though you knew it would be hard, you knew in the end, you would find your joy and happiness.

Every nine seconds in U.S. women are assaulted or beaten

On average nearly 20 people per minute are physically abused by an intimate partner.

One in three women and one in four men have been victims of physical violence by an intimate partner within their lifetime.

One in five women and one in 7 men have been victims of physical severe violence.

On a typical day, there are more than 20,000 phone calls placed to domestic violence hotlines nationwide.

Reader Notes:

_____

_____

_____

_____

_____

_____

_____

_____

_____

_____

_____

_____

_____

_____

_____

_____

_____

_____

_____

_____

_____

_____

_____

_____

_____

_____

_____

_____

_____

_____

_____

_____

_____

_____

_____

_____

_____

_____

_____

_____

_____

_____

_____

_____

_____

Surviving The Abuse
CHAPTER FOUR

It was in the late morning around ten o'clock, the sun was shining and the weather was warm. My husband was sleeping, and I knew that as long as I could keep him asleep, we could make our escape. With knots in my stomach, my nerves in my body shaking and fear in my heart that he would wake up. I asked my oldest son, to quickly start loading up the trunk while I got my other kids together. My son came back in and quietly said, "Mom, the car door is locked, and the keys are in the ignition." My husband had locked the keys in the car on purpose so I couldn't go anywhere at all, while he was asleep. I quietly went into my closet, got the lockout kit, and gave it to my son so he could open the car door. He was able to get the door open, he opened the trunk and started loading up the trunk, with our clothes and blankets we had packed the night before. This was our final move away from my husband. I told the kids to get into the car, and said to my youngest son, we were going to the park for the day. As we drove away, I constantly looked in my rearview mirror, to see if he woke up and tried following us. My hands were sweating, and my heart was racing.

I went to a friend's home, that he didn't know the address too. As we approached my friend's house, I quickly got the kids inside. During our stay there, I would get my kids to school, look for employment and stay as busy as I could to get back on my feet as now as a single mom. We had a new routine in our temporary home, the kids were really good with the new transition. We were able to stay with my friend for about a month, when she had come to me and said that having all of us there was becoming too much for her family. I completely understood. Taking on a family of five is a lot for anyone.

At this time, we had another friend offer us to come and stay with her. We took her up on the kind offer. There wasn't a lot of room at her place, but we had a roof over our head and for that we were grateful. My kids and I stayed there for a couple of months.

I remember it was in the late afternoon, the early evenings were cooler and the nights were cold. My friend and I had an argument, I told my kids to get in the car, and we left, to never return. I drove until I was able to find a safe park set back from the main road. It was a quiet neighborhood park. The kids and I got out of the car, and they played on the playground until nine o'clock. At this time, we became homeless, sleeping from our car to the park benches and grass. The night was cold as I spread the blankets out on the picnic tables for them to rest their head. The grass was too damp from the cold, for them to lay on the ground. I remember sitting next to them, watching them sleep as the tears rolled down my face. I looked up to the sky and prayed to God, to keep us safe, warm and that we wouldn't have to be in this situation for long. I laid my head next to my children, closed my eyes for an hour. I couldn't sleep long as I had to make sure my kids were safe and warm. As I fell asleep with a dream, and I woke with a purpose. I knew there was a different plan God had in store for us. I prayed and prayed for an answer. The very energy you have in pursuing should be the energy you have in prosperity. At times, we would sleep behind churches. The nights were so cold, the grass was wet, the sidewalks were freezing. We did whatever we could at that time to stay warm. My children were still in school. So we would wake up, and go to the nearest gas station, wash up so the kids could be clean for school. When I left my husband, I also left behind the business. I took the little bit of money that I had saved, knowing that eventually I would be leaving. I also knew the money I had put away wouldn't last very long. I would drive my kids to school and looked for a job during those hours. After my kids get out of school we would go back to the park.

We couldn't drive around very much, with the little money we had. When we arrived back to our temporary home (the park) we did homework ate dinner from the food stamps we had, and settled in for the night. The following morning, I would wake the kids up. They would get dressed for school, I would stop at a convenience store for them to wash up before school. Thankfully they were able to eat a warm breakfast at school. Never could I have imagined my life to be like this, even for a temporary situation. I thought I was mentally prepared for what was to come but I wasn't. I don't think anyone ever is.

I continued to stay strong in front of my children. I didn't want them to see me hurting. It was my job as their mom to stay strong. We had survived so much and it was up to me to show them how strong we could be, even in the worst situation we thought, at the time. Even though they could see the pain in my eyes. As a mother, we never expect to be homeless on the streets but we made the best of the situation. I later learned from a counselor it was ok to show my children I was hurting, that it was ok to cry. I wanted them to see that it's healthy to show emotion and to cry, and not keep your feelings all bottled up, and not ever release them.

Two months later there was an opening for a local family shelter. We lived there for three months. How grateful my kids and I were, to finally sleep in a warm and comfortable bed. We had a roof over our head, and somewhere stable for a couple of months. We knew it was temporary, but we were so thankful. To feel the warm water pour over our bodies in the shower, was so refreshing. We were so tired of the washcloth baths we would have to take. It was so wonderful to be able to cook over a stove and provide my children with a warm meal. The search in finding employment continued.

After three months, of being in the shelter, my kids and I received the news that there was an opening for Transitional Living. This would take us out of a shelter, and into another program where we would have our own home. It was more of a stable environment for my family, and things really started looking up for us. Within a couple of months, my car was stolen and totaled. Even though the challenges from this event were somewhat of a setback, life was starting to look more positive. I was back to public transportation, but I was able to land a job! I was finally able to start providing for my family.

Shortly after moving into our new home, is when I started seeing more signs of the abuse that my children went through, come into full effect. The signs of depression and sadness, my children turned to drugs to cope with what they had gone through. They started breaking into people's homes, stealing, and having a loss of self-respect for themselves and everyone around them. My kids quickly became very street smart, from running away from the home often. The police were called many times, giving them warning after warning. It seemed the only way for them to cope with life was to numb themselves with the drugs. Life seemed to turn upside down for us again, as my children tried balancing the rebellious life and school. When my children started breaking into abandoned homes, we got kicked out of the housing program we were a part of. I had two days to pack our things and look for another place to live. After searching for a day, I was able to find another apartment for us to move into. I was so tired of moving and relocating. It was exhausting. It seemed as soon as I got settled in a place for a couple months, even knowing it was a temporary situation, within a couple months I was relocating and having to move somewhere else. I just wanted a place to call my own for a while, and much longer than a couple of months. It had become a normal routine for our family. Many nights I would come home from work, and my kids would be gone. Sometimes they would only be gone for the night, other times it was for a couple days a time. Each time I would call the police to make a report that my kids didn't come home. At times I would have to wait up to three hours, before the officer on duty came to take the report. I knew at this point I needed to increase the counseling sessions my children were in. Now that we have been settled in our new home, and the counseling session has been increased, I was more optimistic that things would start taking a turn for the better. The kids started attending school more often. They seemed to be happier, and I felt like they were finally able to cope with life a little better. My children had learned at an early age on, how to mask their emotions. Just when I thought things were getting better, I quickly learned that my two of my children had thrown a fluorescent light bulb on a someone's door step in the complex we lived in. I asked them why they had done it, and their response was.... I don't know. I sat them down and talked to them, telling them that more than likely we would be getting evicted because of this. With tears streaming down my face, and looking in their eyes as they had no emotion, I asked them, how much longer is this going to continue? They didn't have an answer, we talked a bit more, and then went to bed. When I woke up in the morning before heading out the door for work, I saw a piece of paper taped to my front door. I instantly knew what it was. My stomach instantly went into knots, as I opened the paper to read it. It was a five-day eviction notice. I put the notice on the counter and left for work. Tears still streaming down my face, and so many thoughts going through my mind. I arrived at work and shortly started my search again for another place to move too. Thankfully the eviction hadn't shown up on my credit yet, and I was able to get to another place quickly. With some hope that we might be able to stay, a little longer than two to three months. I had just finished cleaning up from dinner, my phone rang. It was my husband calling to tell me my step son had just gotten a polygraph test done. My husband made sure he told me in detail the abuse his son did to my children and the severity of it all. He was very explicit in detail how many times my children were raped and molested. I couldn't even say good-bye when he finished talking. I dropped the phone, immediately went into the bathroom shut the door, dropped to my knees and cried. I couldn't believe what I had heard! Not just what I had heard, but trying to imagine what my children had gone through. Why was I not there to stop him? Why couldn't I protect my children from this predator? Why were MY children the victims? So many questions entered my mind that night. I felt stupid, dumb, and helpless. My heart was heavier than I had ever experienced before. I stood to my feet and reached above the mirror, and grabbed a razor blade. I turned the water on so no one could hear me and started cutting my arms. This was the beginning of my addiction. I never turned to drugs or alcohol. I turned to cutting. I cut until the pain that was so deep in my heart, was no longer there for the moment. At that moment, I didn't realize that this would be my vice, my escape and my way of coping with certain things in my life. When I cut, it released the pain in that present moment, I was feeling for my children. I learned quickly that this would my way of dealing with any pain, heartache, turmoil or sadness that I would go through. There were times in my life that I cut until I was numb. It didn't matter how many times I cut. I remember counting my cuts after I was done. Each cut had a meaning of a sense of pain I was feeling.

There were times I would cut fifty to seventy-five times before I felt a sense of relief for that moment. I would watch the blood drip from my arms or legs. Wherever I chose to cut at that moment, most of the time is was both. I not only cut to relieve pain. I cut because I suffered from severe depression and anxiety as well. Each scare serves as a reminder of who I am, who I have become, and who must never be again. I wear them proudly because there are some lessons I can't afford to learn again. I would wear long sleeves to cover up my cuts. I didn't want people knowing what was going on. Sometimes if it was too hot outside I would wear quarter length shirts, to hide what I was doing. Going to work each day, with a fake smile on my face to get through what I was personally dealing with. My work peers thought I was so happy all the time, not truly knowing the pain I was suffering deep inside me. I remember many nights feeling overwhelmed from my day, and all I had going on, coming home to my children, getting homework and dinner done. Once my kids were settled in bed, I would be in the shower or bath. It was quiet and it was my time, to reflect on my day and what was going on in my life. This is when I would reach for the razor blade and cut. I cried silently so my children couldn't hear me.

So many times I felt like giving up completely. I would think to myself, maybe if I just took my life, all my pain would go away. In the many thoughts of it, I didn't realize how selfish I was being. I was tired. Tired of fighting. Tired of trying. I didn't want to do it anymore. Three different times I attempted suicide. I felt Each time I stopped for different reasons. I had my kids to live for. My children needed me. I remember a time I was planning my suicide in my head. I was at work and called a friend before I was headed home, told her I was done. I can't keep doing this. What I was feeling that day and thoughts going on in my head, causing so much anxiety, I wanted to be done. I had told her if anything happened to me that night, to make sure my kids were taken care of. I asked her to promise me that she would make sure nothing ever happened to them. She asked me what I was talking about, and I told her if you don't get a call from me tonight, you know I took my life. By the time I got home from work it was late that night. My daughter had prepared dinner for the kids, and they were headed to bed. I remember going to the bathroom, again silently crying, and I started to cut again. This time, lower on my forearm close to my wrist. I wanted it to be over. I didn't want to have to keep on fighting. I heard a knock at the door, it was the police. There were three police officers that came from my friend making a call. My oldest son had answered the door and let them in. My daughter came to the bathroom door and knocked letting me know they were inside. I came out of the bathroom, the officers asked me to come outside so they could talk to me. They didn't want my children hearing what they were talking about. One officer asked me what had happened. Without hesitation, I broke down and cried. I told them what thoughts I was having. The officer says to me; we can't let you stay here tonight. We are going to take you to get some help where you will be admitted for 48 hours. I declined and told them I wasn't going anywhere. He said, "You have two options. You can either go with us and be admitted for forty-eight hours, or we can take you to the mental hospital where they will admit you for two weeks." Of course, I took the shorter option. I get to this facility, where they do an intake with me. Lots of questions were asked, it felt like forever. They placed a wristband on my wrist with the initials DTS (Danger to Self). So that the staff was aware I was suicidal. I hated being in this facility. It gave me so much time to reflect on what I was doing and was a great wake up call for me. There were counselors in there I talked too, the staff was amazing, but I wanted to get home to be with my kids. What was I thinking?

Not only could I not give up on myself, I couldn't give up on my children. I was being selfish for trying to take my life when I was all my children had left. I had to live to tell my story, in hopes to help others who may have lived a similar story, or knew someone that has. My cutting didn't stop, but my attempt at suicide did. At that time, my only outlet I had or felt I had was cutting. Do I still feel like relapsing, knowing that cutting would take away that instant release of whatever I'm going through? Absolutely! But I know now, that cutting isn't the answer. I have learned that talking to someone, and reaching out to my mentors during this time, have helped me tremendously. Until you heal the wounds of your past, you are going to bleed. You can bandage the bleeding with food, with drugs, with alcohol, with anything you want but eventually, it will all ooze through and stain your life. You must find strength to open the wounds, stick your hands inside, pull out the core of the pain that is holding you in your past, the memories and make peace with them. Have you ever been tired of just being tired? If I had to experience what I went through for YOU to endure your pain and depression. It was worth it.

You might be reading this book right now, and might think that people respond differently to depression and abuse. Some binge on alcohol and drugs. They drink or do drugs to numb the pain and sorrow they are feeling. Sometimes we don't inflict pain on ourselves. It's time for you to unmask that pain. It's time for you to stop that pain. Some people mask their pain. It's parallel to habit. Not all habits are bad. Some people will stop doing drugs to start smoking cigarettes. If you find yourself masking the pain, reach out to someone you, you can confide in. Find a mentor. There are so many amazing mentors out there that will help you transition your life in a positive way.

The challenges still continued with my children. Ditching school became so common for them. The Law Enforcement became actively involved. My sleepless night was endless. My son and daughter would run away from home many nights. Not sure if they were safe or where they could be. I was worried sick, and my nights seems longer than hours in the day. I never lost faith that my children would be ok but it was still very scary for me.

One evening while I was at work, I had received a phone call. It was from the Police Officer that was on duty many nights my children ran away. He called and said "I need you to get home right away! I can't tell you over the phone what has happened, but will explain once you're here." At that moment, he didn't give me any information, other than just that. I rushed home, with my heart racing, and my mind worrying. As soon as I pull up to my home, the Officer met me at the gate to let me know my son and daughter had burglarized my neighbor's home. My heart dropped.

I was in complete shock. As I watched my two children get handcuffed and be placed in the back of the Police car, many thoughts ran through my mind. I blamed myself a lot for the choices my children were making. Seeing my kids sitting in the back of the Police car was hard, but I also knew they had consequences for the decisions that they made.

After my children spent three months in jail, my son was sent to a Boys Ranch. My daughter was sent to a group home. I spent my weekends during this time going to visit them. Three hours with my son, and then drive across town to visit my daughter for a couple of hours. My son learned a lot being at the Boys Ranch. He was taught discipline, structure and respect. He attended school every day and played sports. We attended

51

parenting classes together as well. That was very successful, as we were able to build our relationship, and have more of an understanding about the choices he had made prior to him going into the Ranch. It was really good for both of us. He also received the highest award for completing the program. After being in the program for a year, he was able to come home. He was still on probation for a year. Having to do random drug tests each week, to make sure he didn't relapse. The principles he learned while he was at the Ranch, helped him so much. My daughter spent six months in jail and then went into a group home. I was able to visit my daughter once a week at the group home, and over time, she was able to come home on the weekends. As long as her behavior was good at the group home she could spend weekends with me. Our visits were wonderful, and I loved having her home with me. She hated being in the group home. She would attend school, and eventually got a part-time job. I saw the glow in her eyes and the smile on her face when I would drop her off at work and pick her up before taking her back to the group home. She didn't love her job, but she enjoyed getting a paycheck and being able to have a bit of freedom from the group home. Could you imagine getting a phone call late in the night that your son or daughter had run away, and had no idea where they could be? How would you feel and what would you do? That happened to me. One night, I did receive a call from the staff at the group home that my daughter had snuck out the window with another girl in the home in the middle of the night. No one knew where they could be. The police were called, and another report was made. I made several phone calls to friends that I thought she could be with, and no one had heard from her. I drove around looking for her, in hopes to find my daughter. Even though my daughter was street smart I was so scared as to if she was safe, who she may be with, and where she could be. I received a call a couple days later that my daughter was headed to the greyhound, and going to CA. Thankfully the person that contacted me knew what time the bus was leaving. I immediately called the Phoenix Police Department and they dispatched the officers to find my daughter. Luckily they were able to get to her before the bus left. They handcuffed her and took her back to the group home. My daughter was safe thank goodness. I enrolled my son back into a public school, and he was doing really well at home. Attending school, and doing the things I asked of him. I was excited and thought this program was going to be the life changing and turning point for him. I often remind my children; you are who you associate with. He started hanging around with the wrong crowd once again and within a couple of months of him back in school. I get a call from the school that he has been truant from school. Probation was notified and a drug test was given. Because my son had been skipping school and came up dirty on a drug test, he was detained and sent back to jail for another three months. My heart was broken again. I thought for sure we were over this phase and that he would be done with jail. While he was locked up again, I went and visited him once a week. I would walk in through the metal detectors, then check in at the front desk. I would stand in the hallway and wait for the other parents who were there to see their own children. I would watch through the glass, all the juveniles come in a be seated at the tables in the blue chairs. All in different colored shirts, depending on what level they were at with their behavior would determine their shirt color. When the loud buzzer would sound off, for the door to open, the parents would sit across the table from our kids, we weren't allowed to touch them at all. I couldn't hold his hand or hug him. I could only sit and talk with him. I remember the conversations we used to have, many tears were shed, and he would tell me how disappointed in himself he was that he messed up again. He would tell me that when he got out things would be different. He was tired of this lifestyle. After he was released from jail three months later, he was sent to another boy's facility. It was similar to the ranch but different. Instead of the drive to visit only being thirty minutes away, I was driving two hours each way to see him. He was to stay at this facility for three months. He came home and continued with counseling. Each time he came home, I would think to myself... this HAS to be the time he finally gets it. He's going to stay out of jail and things will start to get good. I always thought to myself, my sons had to be tired of this lifestyle.

Let's fast forward a couple of months... It was two weeks before Thanksgiving. It was a Friday night; my daughter was home for the weekend visiting from the group home. I had to work the following morning. My two boys and my daughter were home when I left for work. Imagine coming home from work, to find that half of your son and daughter's clothes are missing and they are gone. Yes, I called the police AGAIN, to report them missing. This time, they were gone for three months. They have never run away this long before. I spent every night reaching out to friends, social media, posting pictures and asking for help in their search. I had an interview with the news, in hopes the news media that SOMEONE would see them around town, or possibly had heard from either one of them.

One evening a bounty hunter saw my kids picture on social media and reached out to me. I met him at a local gas station, less than a mile away from my house. I explained what happened, and how long they had been missing, he took down some information. He stated he wouldn't be able to get on the case for a couple of days since he was working on a different case at the time. We went our separate ways and the following day I received a phone call, that he thought he may have gathered enough evidence that he may know the whereabouts of my children. He told me to stay close to my phone. My heart started beating fast and I started crying with so much joy and hope that they may be safe. He called me that evening and said that he found my children!! He notified the police, to let them know they were found. We waited for the police to get to our location, and they went to the door and found my children. My daughter was hiding in the closet, and my son was hiding under the bed. They were staying at a friend's house who was hiding them out for three months. When the police brought my children out, I just embraced them and cried!! I was so thankful they were safe and ALIVE! and spent many years with my children skipping school, in and out of jail, and in and out of group homes. I often said to myself how long is this phase going to last. At that moment, I knew it wasn't a phase it was a lifestyle. Through all that we went through together, with the challenges we had, I never gave up hope. I never gave up hope of my children. My strength came from the challenges that have been placed in my life. I love the quote by Mother Teresa "God doesn't give us anything we can't handle." So thankful for this quote as it has pulled me through many trials in my life. Have you ever felt trapped in a situation, not sure how to get out? The cuts in my life run deep.

Cuts from abuse, being a victim of sexual abuse and feeling so down I didn't know how I was going to get up. Attempting to take my life three times, were the days I thought suicide was the answer. My last attempt was when I found Hope and purpose in my life. I turn to God for answers and pleaded unto him in despair. It had been a long time since I prayed as hard as I did. My heart was filled with anger, hurt, disappointment, I didn't know what to say. "Heavenly Father, I am so tired. I know you've heard my prayers before. I just don't know what to do. I've tried everything and feel like I keep failing. I feel my purpose in life is much greater than I believe.

With His help and the help of others, I was able to start seeing the light of Hope again. The purpose of moving forward. I would talk to others about their walks of life, and where they came from. It was then that I realized I wasn't alone. I started doing some research and found that the numbers of Domestic Violence and Suicide were large. Did you know that every nine seconds in U.S. women are assaulted or beaten?

There so many people suffering from Darkness and loss of Hope in their eyes and heart. This was the time my healing process started. I had to learn to forgive myself. It was time to cleanse my body, and learn that in order for me to move forward and help others I must go through this process. It was challenging going through so many feelings and emotions, but it was then that I had learned to forgive and let go.

I had to learn to turn the radio off and tune into the motivational material. Motivational Speakers like Les Brown, Orrin Woodward, Jim Rohn, Tony Robbins and Eric Thomas, surrounded me with likeminded individuals. My parents always taught me, you are who you associate with. I wanted to be a writer and a speaker, so that's who I associate with. I attend conferences often, to keep my mind laser focused and keep those positive sources close to me. I realized what my parents went through was their life. It wasn't my life. If you find yourself wanted to cut or drink or even feel like you are at a breaking point, call someone. Turn to someone you can confide in. Know that you're not alone, and there is help out there for you. When I was in this situation of wanting to cut again, I just wanted to have someone that would listen to me. Not judge me or tell me I needed to change, but really just listen and let me cry if I felt I needed too. Instead of dwelling on depression, write a book. Listen to motivational and uplifting speakers. Realize you have other options. I felt like suicide was my only option for a long time. I prayed many times for God to send someone in my path, that could bring some light into this dark place I was in. My prayers were answered. God placed someone in my life, who helped me see another way. I turned the TV off and plugged into positive motivation everywhere I went. Even though I wasn't feeling motivated, this was something I was willing to try anything. I was so tired and consumed from the dark place in my life I had been living in for so long. I am thankful today and every day that God's plan for me was and still is bigger than I ever imagined. Do you ever feel like the weight of the world or just simply LIFE is weighing so heavy on your heart and your shoulders, and you feel like giving up? If you ever feel your life isn't worth living, and you can't move forward. It's easy to give up, but you can't give up on the thousands of lives who are waiting to hear your story. If you feel like money and stress is the only vehicle, there are other options. When you're having a bad day, say to yourself. "I'm doing this for this person. Give your WHY a name. WHY are you doing resisting temptation for that person? I was my own bully by cutting myself up because the bully kept telling me, I was weak. I wasn't worth living. The bully inside me convinced me that I didn't have a purpose in life anymore, and I wasn't listening to God tell me how strong I was. I had to believe what God was telling me. I continued to listen to affirmations daily. I prayed every day for the strength to be strong. When I wanted to cut I went for a walk or called a friend, and prayed to God for the strength to overcome what was inside me that made me so weak.

No, I will never forget what happened in my life, but learning to forgive, and going through the process I have had to learn to adapt and remember who I am doing this for. I was being selfish and doing it because I didn't want to have a broken family. I always thought things will get easier and better over time. Things will change, but it never got better it only got worse. I was torn down daily which then led to zero self-worth. No self-esteem and wanting to break the cycle by leaving. It was after me leaving and coming back to the same relationship that continued abuse pain and destruction that I knew I couldn't keep putting my family through. I have learned to adapt to it by being raised with a father who was abusive to my mom. I knew it wasn't normal and often wondered how I adapted to the situation myself. It was later that I learned all the faith I need, is the faith of a mustard seed. I learned this from a lady by the name of Desiree Lee. The author of "Inmate 1142980: The Desiree Lee Story". Who taught me a great lesson. She said "With a mustard seed of faith you can move mountains. This is ALL the faith you need." It was really all the faith I had left. When God spoke and said, "Let there be light," it was so. For our words are vibrations, vibrations are energy, energy is power. So speak to your mountains and they will MOVE! Speak to your problems and they will MOVE! Speak to your fear and it will MOVE! Speak to your doubt and it will MOVE! There is power in your words and when we recognize this authority that lives within us, the

61

authority to create and destroy, the authority to speak life or death, the authority to speak that very dream into existence, then and only then will you overcome the very thing is stifling you from stepping into your greater, from stepping into your purpose that God has placed inside of you." Dream so big, that when it happens you know it's not you.

Reader Notes:

How were you able to overcome an obstacle in your life, where you wouldn't allow the inner bully to consume your thoughts and actions?

_____

_____

_____

_____

_____

_____

_____

_____

_____

_____

_____

_____

_____

_____

_____

_____

_____

Excelling, The Final Cut

CHAPTER FIVE

If the wounds on her heart, and the bruises on her soul, were translated on her skin, you wouldn't have recognized her at all. I know that God didn't have it in His plan to live a life full of sorrow, sadness or depression. Yes, we will go through life with hard times and challenges, to make us stronger. We are to live a life of purpose. What is your purpose? Are you living to the fullest? Are you dreaming so big that your dreams scare you? If not, I encourage you to dream bigger! Maybe you're going through some challenges in life where you feel like you've lost hope. You are feeling like life isn't worth pressing forward. Don't give up! Keep pushing! You aren't alone. Even on the darkest of days and nights, I encourage you to get on your knees and pray. Pick up the phone and call SOMEONE. Giving up isn't the answer. After attempting suicide three times, I thank God every day His plan was and still is much bigger than I ever imagined. If you don't believe it, YOU TRULY MATTER! You do! Your feelings matter. Your voice matters. Your story matters and your LIFE matters.

Don't let someone who doesn't know your value, tell you how much your worth. I am learning to Rise Up and not be afraid to use my voice. I have gone from wounded to worthy of being able to have the of what others are or have experienced. I was understanding put on this earth to be great, and that's exactly what I'm going to be. What you see determines what you say. What you say determines where you stay. Where you stay determines what you believe. What you believe determines the level of your faith.

I have been victimized. I was in a fight that was not in a fair fight. I did not ask for the fight, I lost. There is no shame in losing such fights. I have the stage of survivor and am no longer a slave of victim status when I look back with sadness rather than hate, I look forward with hope, rather than despair. I may never forget, but I need not constantly remember. I was a victim. I am a survivor! You too can be a survivor! Don't be another statistic in the books. Learn to find your voice and help be the voice of those afraid to speak out. If I hadn't found my voice, I wouldn't be able to share my journey, impact the lives of others and receive emails from those that I helped along the way, if I chose to not speak out, and share my journey. I recently received an email from someone, that shared with me, at this time when he came across one of my messages on social media, he was at one of the lowest points of his life. He mentioned that because of what I said and the inspiration of hope I had given him at that time, was the reason he didn't give up. I was the reason he continued to press forward in life, and he is now inspiring others. His WHY is his children, but because of where he was in his life, it was hard to keep fighting for his why, until we crossed paths. As I have mentioned before, you never know who's watching you, and who is waiting to hear your story. Your journey isn't for everyone, but it is for someone, and when that someone here's it. You will know. I know you may feel as if giving up is the answer, throwing in the towel seems so much easier than fighting for your life, but you've got to keep fighting. So many lives are needing to be impacted and saved. You may be that person that someone is waiting to hear from. You are important and you matter! Your voice matters, your Story matters, and your LIFE matters. Don't let someone who doesn't know your value, tell you how much your worth.

Reader Notes:

Describe a situation you were able to excel in your life and not have to hurt anymore.

_____

_____

_____

_____

_____

_____

_____

_____

_____

_____

_____

_____

_____

_____

_____

_____

_____

_____

_____

_____

_____

_____

_____

_____

_____

_____

_____

_____

_____

_____

_____

_____

_____

_____

_____

_____

_____

_____

_____

_____

_____

_____

About The Author

Lisa Halls

Author | Public Speaker | Philanthropist

Lisa Halls a native of Mesa, Arizona. Ms. Halls has been on numerous radio shows sharing the journey of her story. Inspiring multiple Domestic Violence Survivors nationwide to eliminate fear, and obtain the courage to find their voice during traumatic experiences. She continues to coach hundreds of people worldwide, through her inspiration during various talks to audiences.

Her limitless energy and confidence impacts her clients to break down fear and lead on a global level. From writing a book "The Cuts Don't Hurt Anymore" From Abuse to Abundance to inspiring others, she's one influencer to watch. Ms. Halls has a personal mission in life to inspire individuals who feel they can't overcome their current barriers. She stands as a reminder to those who come into her presences, to never give up.